A MACDONALD BOOK

Text © 1988 Angela Littler
Illustrations © 1988 Macdonald & Co (Publishers) Ltd

First published in Great Britain in 1988
by Macdonald & Co (Publishers) Ltd
London & Sydney

A member of Maxwell Pergamon Publishing Corporation plc

Printed and bound in Spain by Cronion S.A.

ISBN 0 356 13499 7
ISBN 0 356 16033 5 pbk

Macdonald & Co (Publishers) Ltd
Greater London House
Hampstead Road
London NW1 7QX

Touching and Feeling

Written by Angela Littler

Illustrated by Corinne Burrows

Macdonald

Touching

When I touch something . . .

I can tell if it is hot

I can tell if it is cold

I can tell if it is wet

I can tell if it is dry

I can tell if it is rough

I can tell if it is smooth

How?

Feeling

I can feel tickles

I can feel itches

I can feel bumps

I can feel cuts and grazes

I can feel bruises

I can feel hot

I can feel cold

How?

5

How I feel and touch

Dotted around my body there are tiny feeler spots called receptors. They are much too small to see. Some receptors tell if things are hot or cold. Some are good at touching. Some tell me when things press me or hurt me. Some bits of me are better at feeling or touching things than others.

My eye feels pain easily. It really hurts when I get something in it.

My elbow is good at feeling hot things. It is not good at touching.

My toenails cannot feel anything. It does not hurt to cut them.

My hair cannot feel anything at all.

My cheek can feel the slightest touch.

My fingertips are good at touching.

7

Why does it hurt?

Pain is not nice, but it is very useful. It tells us straightaway if something is wrong.

We sometimes feel pain inside our bodies. It helps us to take care of ourselves by telling us when we are ill.

Getting hot and cold

When we feel very hot, our skin starts to sweat. As the sweat dries on our skin, it makes us feel cooler.

When we feel very cold, we get goose pimples. The hairs on our body are fluffing out to keep us warm — like birds' feathers.

Hair and nails

Nails and hair are made out of a special hard stuff that also grows in our skin. It is called keratin.

My nails cannot feel anything. It does not hurt to cut them.

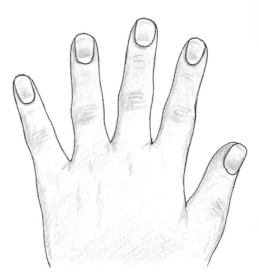

There are no receptors in keratin so our hair and nails do not feel anything.

Scales, hoofs, and claws are made of keratin too.

Hard puzzle

All these hard parts of animals are made out of keratin. Do you think they can feel? Do you know the names of the parts?

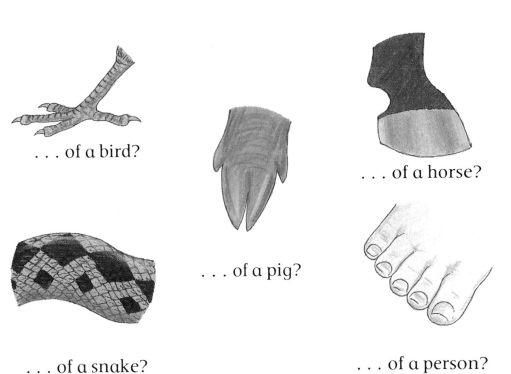

. . . of a bird?

. . . of a pig?

. . . of a horse?

. . . of a snake?

. . . of a person?

Test yourself for touch

Touch your nails and your hair gently with a fine paintbrush. Can they feel anything?

Touch your palm gently with the paintbrush. Does it tickle?

Now touch your elbow with the paintbrush. Can you feel it at all? Does it tickle?

Q: Where do you have more touch receptors: your palm or your elbow?

A: Your palm.

The hair test

Take one hair from your head and touch your cheek as gently as you can. Can you feel it?

Now touch all over the top of your arm with the hair. Sometimes you cannot feel it at all.

Q: Where do you think you have more receptors: your cheek or your arm?

A: Your cheek.

Animals . . .

Animals like rabbits, mice, hamsters and cats have whiskers. Whiskers look like our hairs, but they can feel things. They tell animals if spaces are big enough for them to get through.

Some animals, like frogs and tortoises, cannot bear the cold. They go to sleep for the whole winter. This is called hibernating.

and their itches and twitches

Flies make horses itch and twitch. So they swish their tails to keep the flies away. Sometimes, two horses stand head to tail. This way the tails stop the flies from bothering their heads too.

Chimpanzees care for each other by picking itchy fleas and insects out of each other's fur.

Hot and cold puzzle

In a faraway country live two people. One person lives on a mountain. It is cold and wet. The other person lives down where it is hot and dry.

The two people have got everything muddled.
Each person has ten things that the other one
needs. Can you spot them?

A: The cold person needs: hot drink, duvet, blanket,
mackintosh, heater, moon boots, scarf, woollen hat, thick
coat, umbrella. The hot person needs: swimsuit, cool drink,
refrigerator, parasol, sun-hat, ice cream, paddling pool,
sunglasses, flip-flops, fan.

17

Feely bag

Take turns with a
friend to fill a shoe bag
or strong paper bag
with everyday things.
The other person has to
guess what the things
are, just by feeling
them.

Here are some ideas for your feely bag:

apple	spoon	orange
toothbrush	cork	carrot
sock	hard biscuit	hard tomato
clean potato	plastic mug	sponge
lemon	or cup	rubber
glove	tissue	banana

Remember: Never put anything sharp or
dangerous in your feely bag.

Feely collection

Use an old cereal box to make this collection.
Divide it into four with paper strips. Look for soft
things like feathers, cotton wool and dandelion
clocks. Find hard things like old keys, pencils,
buttons and building blocks. Collect rough things
like bark and sandpaper, and smooth things like
pebbles and silky fabric.

The cave

Sally, Ted, Bob and Ann spent the day at the beach with their mother. In the afternoon, they played ball. Somehow, Ann's glasses got broken. Ann could hardly see without her glasses. Mum was very angry with them all.

"Now just sit still and behave yourselves – and look after Ann!" she said.

So the children sat quietly and got very bored. Mum was reading a book. Slowly, she dropped off to sleep. The naughty children crept off to play.

They found a deep cave, and dared each other to go inside. Deeper and deeper into the cave they went, until suddenly, they realised they were lost. They could not remember the way out, and it was too dark in the cave to see anything.

They thought they were lost for ever. Little Ted began to cry. But then Ann said,

"It's all right. I know the way back."

"How can you, Ann?" asked Bob. "It's so dark and you can hardly see without your glasses anyway."

"No, but I can *feel* things!" said Ann. "I remember when we came in I felt the wet splash of a waterfall.

Then I felt the softness of a sandy floor under my feet. Then we clambered over some hard, jagged rocks. Then there was a path of wet, slippery mud. If we follow these things backwards, we should be able to find our way out."

And they did.

Can you see which way they went?